Haiku
Gold

Verses by
Paul Amphlett

Edited by Frank Thynne

Haiku Gold

Verses

by Paul Amphlett

Edited by Frank Thynne

Published by Peer Poetry International
21 Stall Street, Bath BA1 1QF, England

ISBN: 978-0-9926996-0-4

Foreword by the Editor

"Gold" appears in the title of this short anthology because it reflects the value that poets and readers ascribe to Haiku. To convey so much meaning into a short verse is an enjoyable challenge to the poet and it appeals to readers familiar with the form and those encountering it for the first time.

The roots of Haiku lie in poetry written to entertain the Court in China and Japan. Later, in the 17th century Bashō settled on a form that in the Western world is represented by a verse in three lines of five, seven and five syllables. The form has become so popular that the work of Bashō and his followers has been translated into many languages and much modern Haiku is written in English.

The traditional pattern of a Haiku verse begins with a static or continuous situation, followed by an event or action leading to a conclusion – often surprising or at least thought-provoking. If you can see two or more different interpretations then so much the better!

Some writers follow the 5-7-5 syllable rule strictly, in which each of the three elements occupies exactly one line. However, even Bashō occasionally ventured beyond the formal pattern of his day and many poets today feel that the 5-7-5 form should be respected but not constrain the writing of effective Haiku. Punctuation, irrelevant to the Japanese form, may be used as well as or instead of line endings to distinguish the three elements.

Each Haiku verse stands and can be enjoyed by itself. Do not try to read too many verses at one time - rich food should be eaten in small portions.

In Paul Amphlett's Haiku you will find brevity and wit often with, in his own words, a twist at the end. Some will make you think, others will make you happy or sad, and some will make you laugh out loud. The verses in this book are just a few of many that Paul has written and which we expect to publish later. It has been a joy to work with Paul in preparing them for publication. We have laughed together and agonised together over finding the best of two or three different versions of a verse and hope that you will enjoy the result.

lunch; suffering
the attentions of a wasp:
to a beef pie

friend's advanced age:
our slightest contact
painful

"so sorry" - smiled,
breast brushed his arm:
"my pleasure"

a swat required:
that fly followed me
no packed lunch

ripe gooseberries:
sticky fingers
sheer delight

the service complete:
a thorny rose to throw
... he'd thrown in the towel

flat roof:
after the storm, blotch spreads
'twixt here and heaven

slumped on her knees:
sequins still hurt...
too many drinks

amongst bare branches:
silhouetted faces
snarl and threaten

Sunday, empty:
the worst part - another day
without her letter

ancient aunt:
painful visit; nearly dropped
her fixed smile

balloon's shadow:
elegant oval glides
over rough terrain

black holes:
punched in white dew, remains
of dog's early run

Blackpool Tower Zoo:
viewing animals carefully,
captured - uncaged girls

twins, entertaining:
bounding bosoms -
supermarket dancers
(New Zealand)

Bob's chosen award:
bounding up the beach -
my unwelcome shower

girl violated -
an unclean caress
swerves from behind

sardines prepared:
crowd upon crowd
of seabirds

feeble old lady:
startled thought;
retraces her steps

dog's stone skimming:
ripples spread
w i d e r - smaller

butterfly, fluttering:
randomly, everywhere -
finally settles

Eze cacti garden:
impaled by many spikes
I sprawl many steps

cake stall ignored:
ample girl shakes her head...
pats her stomach

mentally chased:
by terrifying cloud of
Twin Tower debris

chasing the wind:
to my gate; downpour arrived
after our dog

wishful parents:
fractious child
screeches again

clean mirror:
from just one angle
smeared

start to 'drop off':
drowsy thoughts of travels
overcooked chicken!

clearing debris:
after the explosion -
burying blood and khaki

threatened, clear sky:
Sun, dislodged for a moment
by wispy cloud

the cicada:
as I get closer
silence falls

complete surprise:
to find a news report
wholly accurate

starving anxious squab:
defiant amongst the rubbish,
dashes free

crowded path:
accustomed pigeon weaves,
snatching crumbs

new moon:
earthlight circle seen
within its horns

crude statue:
looks
much heavier

by the grate:
scuffling for the future
boisterous, my man-cubs

deaf girl's face:
brusquely leaves flower market
shouting, in furious signs

deceptive screen:
until the print-out unfurls
mistakes revealed!

sun-brushed:
mackerel clouds
shine in your eyes

at her pub exit:
glass crunched underfoot,
distorted face glares

mother, distraught:
her child shrills at his dog
busy dangerous street

disused rail station:
acrid smoke reminder
'all aboard!'

an ant at the top:
tumbles down a sand hill
once more

dragonfly:
flashes along the stream,
sips now and then

snow, lightly descending:
cherry-blossom's intermittent fall,
a young girl passes away

early evening -
Venus shines: if you know where
to observe

garden stroll:
dozens of shining trails -
slugs already arrived

favourite hours:
time for cuddles and kisses
slow mutual orgy

entering the 'loo':
"can I go first?"
child's unwelcome cry

some distance away:
entering my nostrils
smell of the ocean

entering the ward:
a deliberate smile
disguises my tears

misgiving: faint light
vanishing, rattle
in the Tube

splayed insect, helpless:
prismatic rings
float down-stream

faithful servant:
finished work
finished him

philatelist: seems
more curious about the stamp
than the contents

humming alone:
beginning to irritate me;
same tune each morning

finding fair 'pussy':
has so many cherished -
connotations

foot and mouth - legs
poke above the fire:
bent, farmer's shoulders

forced to switch off:
a Parliamentary answer -
blasted phone advert!

deathbed:
old artist surveys once more
his favourite view

Wells:
no suburbs, countryside
commences next street

from the cemetery;
imprints shape a snowy path -
towards the shops!

black moraine:
creeps up the glacier
in the sun's heat

girl's silent laugh:
delicious with secrets
as her skirts flare up

glacier melt
deluges snow-capped boulders:
tumbling whitecaps

half-awake at night:
uneasily conscious of
Jane's drowsy groans

half-naked girl
covered in mud: soaking wet,
copy of Vogue style

hammer blow:
auctions uncaring my years -
linchpin memories

horror novel:
on the page, tiny death moves;
deadly caterpillar

common dormouse:
nowadays, with insecticides
uncommon dormouse

hot days, cool shade:
how her body undulates
under loving hands

failing to remember
what I've failed
to remember

hotel? - Hammerfest:
sailors, girls, tramps – girls laugh
on the stairs together

hot water runs over:
smart youngster skedaddles,
won't be involved

in a great hurry:
bounced athletically from
bra-cup to bra-cup

Aussie sky:
someone else's Milky Way
spans the horizon

squeak:
branches twist,
a slight wind

sad slug display:
no beauty contest;
leave it to the snails

at this hospital:
'nil by mouth'
welcome

intrigued by the plot:
reading very late, wrecked
my internal clock

plane passes low:
lecturers climax
swamped –soundless

invalid's last walk:
in her beloved garden
a late rose blooms

as the kite soars:
familiar creases crinkle –
old fellow's eyes

exhausted kitten
on my palm: puppy's tail wags -
just playing

legal jargon:
filling funeral forms
why not black taped death?

peacefully at dusk:
the dew descends, settles
on moss - en masse

hunkered down kitten:
muscles poised to leap -
on a stag beetle!

sliding hand
on silken skin:
meets a fur barrier

long-drawn wait:
expectation fades,
letter on the mat

for an hour or so:
ephemeral elegance,
overnight frost

lying in bed
as the wind rises: creaks
and groans everywhere

front of the bus:
man splutters - again,
flu germs, free

many a swallow:
makes a summer
for a python

hints a lot later:
cherished book returned,
after the wake

aquarium flow:
sad sea anemone
filtered favourite

mists swirl:
longed-for destination
appears - vanishes

ambition – hope!
stream washes onward to
broken water-wheel

knowing eyes:
meet and explore intimately
the space between us

favourite cake
one slice left:
stale...

mist swirls, leaves drip:
glints of light
stab shadowed water

new 'Jerseys':
flavour even stronger
in my cold salad

morning hills
swathed in mist: or
misted window-panes?

now spitting fire:
Catherine wheel,
shortly, all twisted

horizon reviewed:
however far I walk -
it comes no closer

oak trees below:
band of mist, beyond – above,
Glastonbury Tor

horror
of Chechnya: hostages
and their parents

lumpy porridge:
in the food processor –
now, creamy porridge

religious hospital:
'passeth all understanding' –
the food here

only the news:
makes this lovely day
unbearable

my coat sleeve:
a snowflake wonder –
soon a drop of water

imagine, daily:
into the sea, incredible
amounts of sewage

enjoyable silence:
cat's caterwauling surprise...
smiling, we laugh

typist's chair:
surrounded by evidence:
cake crumbs

winter romance:
factory steam wavers
into bitter blue

peaceful landscape:
gardener at work; the lady's
frown harbours a storm

lengthy life class:
model bored with the pose
we yawn

pink parchment:
his name roughly erased
from the letterhead

distorted:
plane tree trunk
by parasitic wen

sobbing: pregnant girl
outside the pharmacy, late -
locked door reopened

prenuptial lawyers:
in case, smooth
the 'plight path'

railway museum:
a lovely old 'puffer'
blew its nose – briefly

rainbow switched
on and off:
by passing clouds

shelter:
messed homework
school excuse

rest room:
clattering, chattering,
mobile gossip

underestimated:
realising "free love"'s
expensive

returned:
to give a vagrant money;
get back his smile

for an hour or so:
ephemeral elegance,
overnight frost

salt sea air: one tug;
kite and heart
swoop together

same cremation image:
cancer - burns all three wives
as if together

proud to show:
all those lovely white teeth -
proud of her toothpaste

shrieking white gulls:
a constant mantle
covers the holm

shut out by winter:
but ice, spites every effort,
silent, creeps in

a shoal of fry:
a careless move; as one,
they turn in the stream

mass graves, desolate:
slogans not required -
sightseers?

cliff shadows, austere:
sun's aspect changes,
face frowns

dealing with the post:
half an hour's work recycles
wasted material

sound of perfection:
as the opener's bat
strikes the ball

a quick read:
must get to the end
3 pm already

mists surround:
pale autumn moon
your cold lips

quiet path ahead:
resigned to loneliness,
everything recedes

just a few flakes:
tiny rodent tracks erased
by a cat's paw

cliff point:
a light from sheeted clouds
glows on seamen's graves

last step tricky:
aged lady with a stick
falters – arms offered

baby: observed
sticks out its tongue
at a passer-by

sour in the mouth:
grub's nest
open to the skies

"bad fire – no one there:
lost two fine dogs,
oh .. er .. and our butler"

www.ingramcontent.com/pod-product-compliance
Ingram Content Group UK Ltd.
Pitfield, Milton Keynes, MK11 3LW, UK
UKHW020231250726
13967UKWH00001B/298